It's OK to Cry

It's OK to Cry

Copyright © 2020 by Hunter Dan

All rights reserved. No part of this publication may be reproduced, distributed, or transmitted in any form or by any means, including photocopying, recording, or other electronic or mechanical methods, without the prior written permission of the author, except in the case of brief quotations embodied in critical reviews and certain other noncommercial uses permitted by copyright law.

Paperback: 978-1-6455054-2-6

Matchstick Literary
3000 Atrium Way
Suite 200 - PMB 20019
Mt. Laurel, NJ 08054-3910
info@matchliterary.com
www.matchliterary.com

It's OK to Cry

By Hunter Dan

Illustrations By Pam Hodgdon

Dedicated to Pam's dad, Ben Brown. His love of his family, service to his country and dedication to every facet of his life made him a popular man around town. His life and passing was the inspiration to this story.

My name is Timmy. I like reading, riding my bike and playing with my dog Maisy. My favorite thing to do is play toss with my Grampa Ben.

Grampa Ben lives next door. When I get home from school every day, he is there to greet me. He gives me a hug and says "wanna play ball?"

We play toss with a baseball, football, we shoot baskets and we kick my soccer ball.

My dad works late so Grampa Ben is there everyday to play with me. Next to Maisy, he is my best friend.

Sometimes after supper while mom and dad are watching TV, Grampa Ben and I will go outside and lay on the lawn and look up at the stars. He taught me the big dipper, the little dipper and the north star. One night we even saw a falling star.

We talk about everything. He has taught me so much. I know I'm only 7 years old but I don't know what I would do without him.

Today is Thursday and It started out like every other day. I went to school, I walked home like I do every day. Except when I got home my mom and dad were there waiting for me, not Grampa Ben.

Where is Grampa Ben? I asked. They sat me down and said, "we need to talk to you about Grampa Ben." I could tell something was wrong.

Timmy, something happened to Grampa Ben today, my dad said. What happened? I asked. His heart stopped working my dad said. With tears in his eyes, he said, "he didn't make it."

I don't understand, where is he? Why wasn't he here when I got home? My dad said, "he went to the hospital in the ambulance. The doctors tried to save him but they couldn't. He passed away."

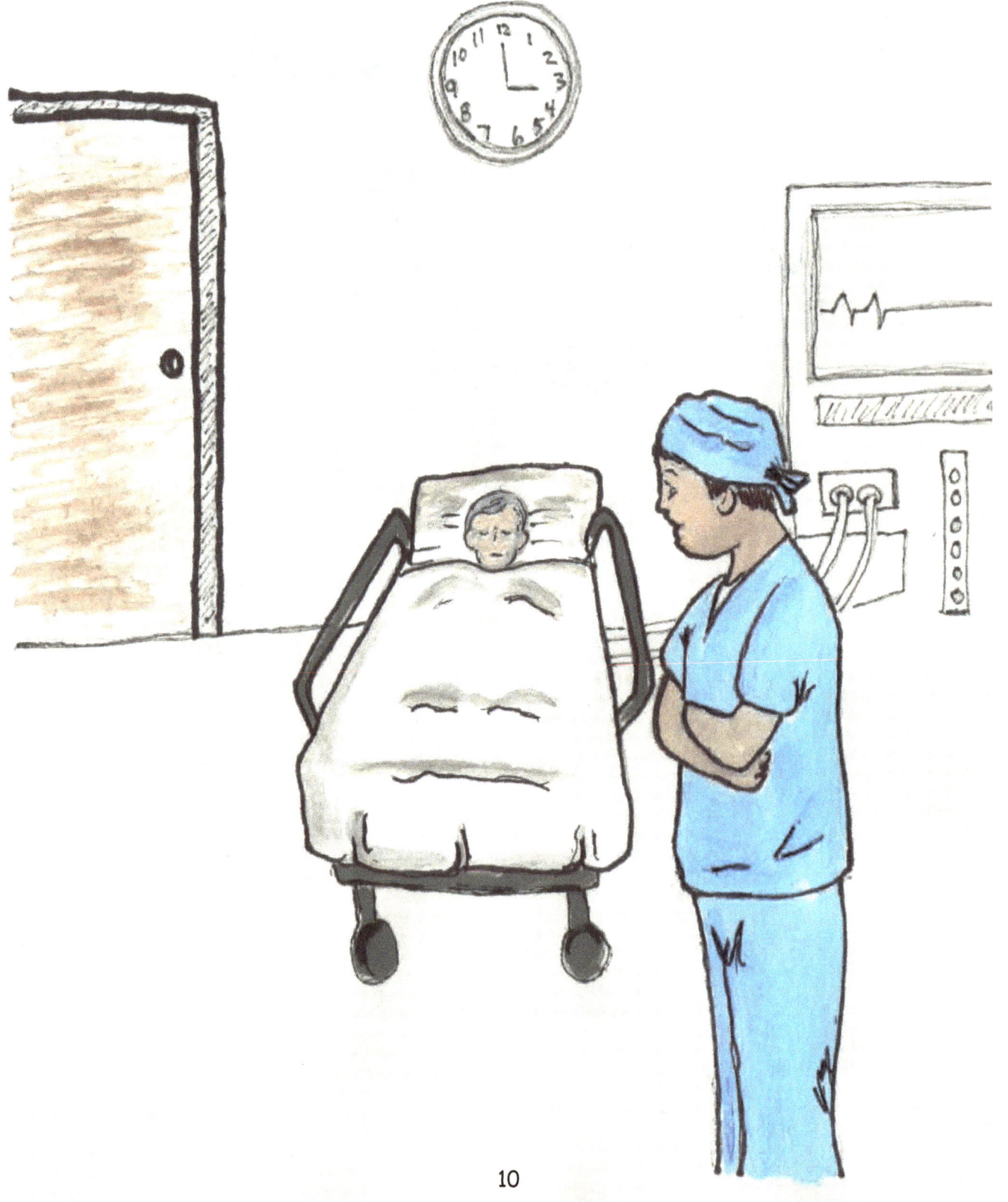

Passed away? You mean he went to heaven? Yes, my dad said. I didn't know what to say, I don't know how to feel. Grampa Ben told me about heaven. He said it was a magical place. That everybody when they die, this is where they go.

He told me it is up above the clouds. When you go there your spirit is free. There is no pain, there is no suffering. Even pets go there. They watch over us and we would be able to feel their presence. That we can talk to them, we just can't see them.

My mom and dad hugged me and said they were sorry. Why are you sorry? I asked. Grampa Ben told me he wasn't afraid to go there. He would see all of his friends and he would see his mom and dad.

Grampa Ben told you all about this? My mom asked. Yes, I said, last week when we looked at the stars he told me all about heaven. I asked him how he knows all this and he said, "I know because I have faith."

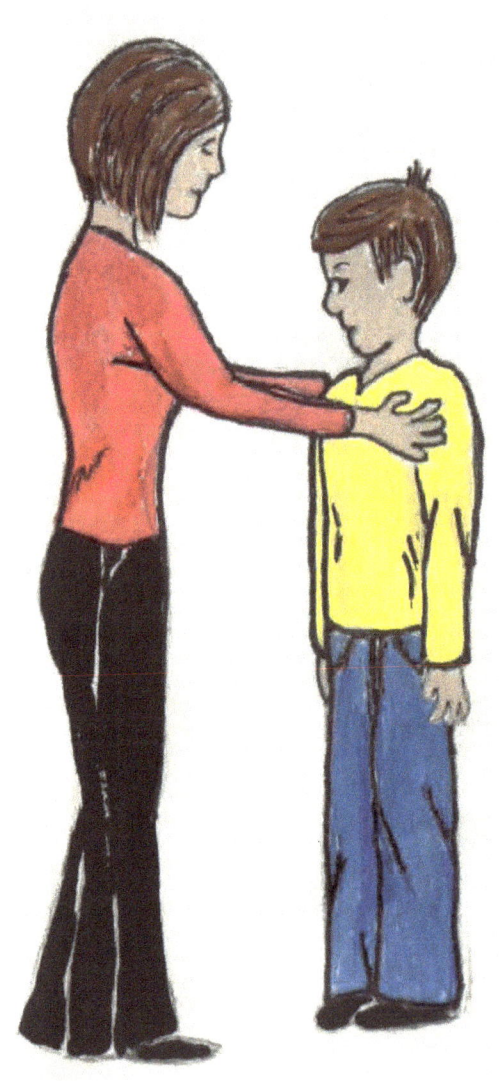

He also said that it's not the end for them. For them it's a new beginning. For us, we will always have the memories of the good times we had with them.

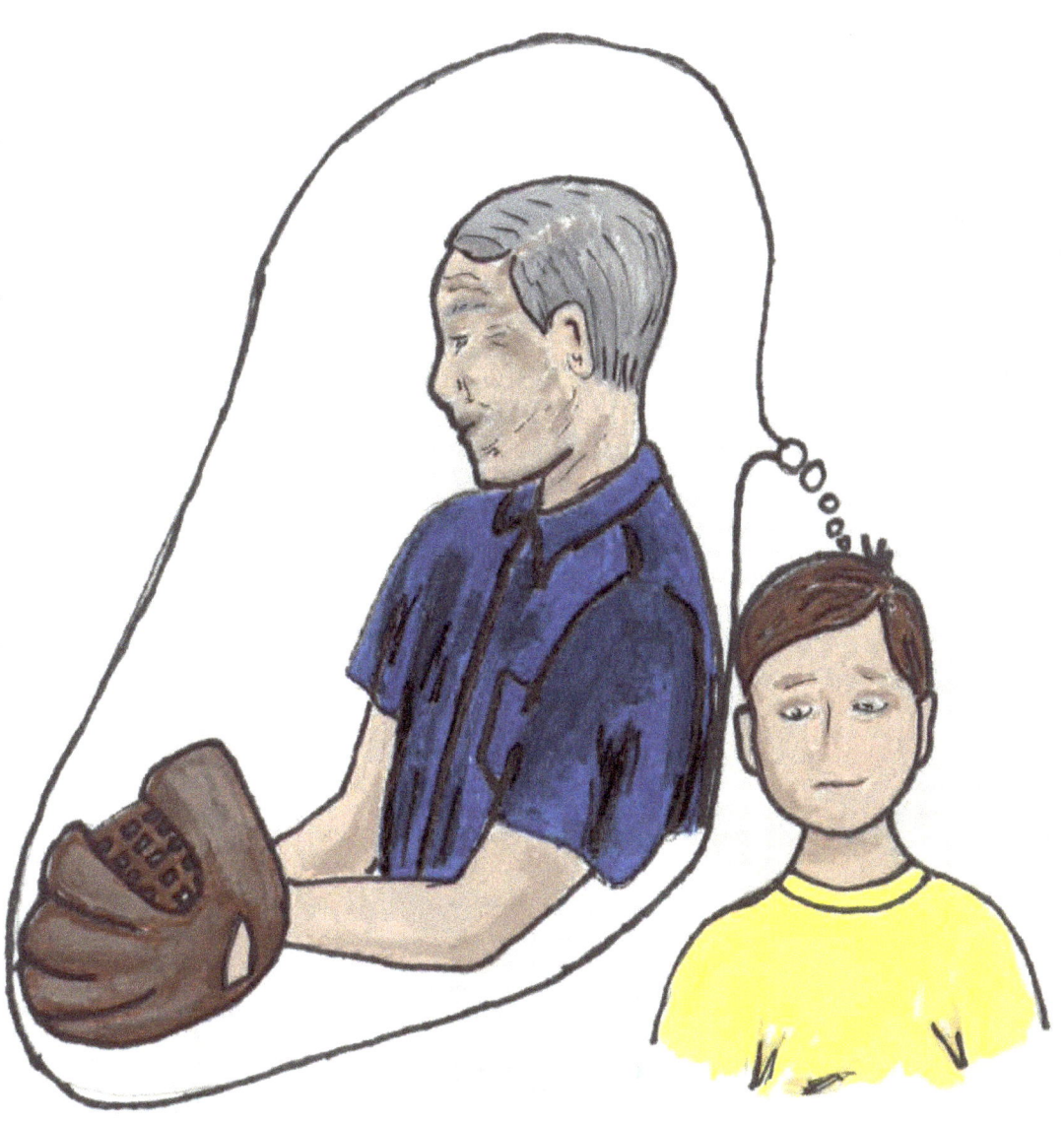

But I guess this means I will never see him again. How is that possible? He was here every day when I got home from school. I am going to miss him.

It has been a long four days. Now it's Monday and I am tired. People were calling, coming to visit and dropping off food. Today is the funeral. Dad said, "this is when we say goodbye to Grampa Ben. We are celebrating his life and all the good he brought into our lives."

Dad explained to me that Grampa Bens body is in the casket but his soul is in heaven looking down on us. He can't feel pain but he knows we are sad.

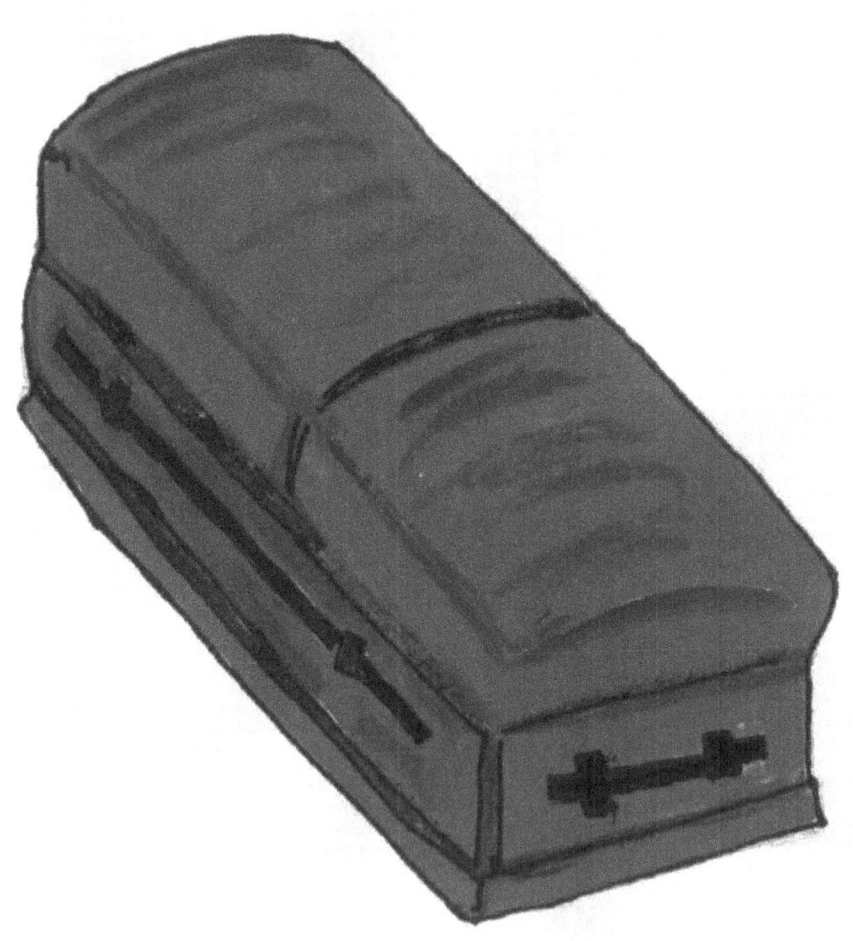

After the service, my mom, dad and I waited for everyone else to say goodbye. Some people were crying. Now it's time for us to say good bye. We walked up to the casket, they put their hands on it, so I put my hand on it too.

My heart hurts. I looked at my dad. With tears in his eyes, he said, "Its OK to cry."

My eyes welled with tears. I looked at Grampa Ben and said, "here is my baseball so we can play toss when I get to heaven. I know you will always be with me and watching over me. I will never forget you, good bye for now, I love you Grampa Ben!"

www.ingramcontent.com/pod-product-compliance
Lightning Source LLC
Chambersburg PA
CBHW061146070526
44584CB00033B/4440